Library

By Jennifer Colby

21st Century Junior Library

Published in the United States of America by
Cherry Lake Publishing
Ann Arbor, Michigan
www.cherrylakepublishing.com

Content Adviser: Lucy Wines, Youth Services Librarian
Reading Adviser: Marla Conn MS, Ed., Literacy specialist, Read-Ability, Inc.

Photo Credits: ©Susan Chiang/iStock Images, cover, 1, 10; © mattomedia Werbeagentur/Shutterstock Images, 4; © wavebreakmedia/Shutterstock Images, 6, 8, 18; © Monkey Business Images/Shutterstock Images, 12; © Tyler Olson/Shutterstock Images, 14, 16; © Jason Doiy/iStock Images, 20

Library of Congress Cataloging-in-Publication Data
Names: Colby, Jennifer, 1971- author.
Title: Library / by Jennifer Colby.
Description: Ann Arbor : Cherry Lake Publishing, [2016] | Series: 21st century junior library. Explore a workplace | Includes bibliographical references and index.
Identifiers: LCCN 2015048515| ISBN 9781634710756 (hardcover) | ISBN 9781634712736 (pbk.) | ISBN 9781634713726 (ebook) | ISBN 9781634711746 (pdf)
Subjects: LCSH: Libraries—Juvenile literature. | Library employees—Juvenile literature. | Library science—Vocational guidance—Juvenile literature.
Classification: LCC Z665.5 .C65 2016 | DDC 027—dc23
LC record available at http://lccn.loc.gov/2015048515

Cherry Lake Publishing would like to acknowledge the work of The Partnership for 21st Century Learning. Please visit *www.p21.org* for more information.

Printed in the United States of America
Corporate Graphics

CONTENTS

You can find books about many subjects at the library.

What Is a Library?

You walk past shelves of books. You need information for a school project. Aha! You find the books you need. They are organized by subject. Now you must check them out. Where are you? You are at the library.

Many libraries have computers for you to use.

Some people **borrow** books, music, and movies at the library. Others use computers. Many people want a quiet spot to study and read. The library is a great place to learn new things.

Create!

Draw a map of your library. Show your favorite areas. Do you like the story area? Do you like to use the computers? Draw the person who helps you in the library.

Library workers like to help people.

Library Workers

Where can you find your favorite book? Who do you ask if you need help on the computer? Library workers are happy to help! They want you to find what you need. Let's learn about library workers!

Librarians like sharing books with children.

Librarians have many jobs in a library. They help you find books. They help you with online **research**. Some librarians work only with children. They read stories to kids just like you. All librarians hope you find the information you need at the library.

This librarian is choosing new books for the library.

Libraries have many interesting books. Librarians choose books that you will enjoy reading. They also order books that will help you learn. Librarians work hard to make sure there is something for everyone at the library.

Look!

Along with books, libraries have many different things for you to enjoy. Can you name other items that you borrow or use? Here's a hint: You can listen to some things you check out from the library.

Clerks use scanners to check items in and out.

There are many other workers at a library. **Clerks** help you check out items from the library. They also check in items that you return. They use a **scanner** to check books in and out.

Do you need a **library card** to check out a book? How can you get one? A clerk can help you sign up for a card.

Shelvers make sure bookshelves are neat.

Who else works at a library? There are workers to help you with computers. There are **shelvers** who **sort** books. They put books in the right spot on library shelves. A library will also have a **director**. This person is in charge of all the workers.

A library needs many workers. They want to make it easy for you to find information and learn. They also want you to have fun! They hope you will come back soon.

Library workers are happy to answer questions about their jobs.

Do You Want to Work at a Library?

Would you like to work at a library? Would you like to be a librarian? Would you like to help people with computers?

Talk to library workers. Ask them about their jobs. You might find out that library workers like reading. Or they might like helping people find information.

It is important for library workers to be friendly and welcoming to all library visitors.

How can you prepare for a job at the library? Read lots of books to become a good reader. You should also know how to use computers.

A library is a fun place to work. Find out as much as you can now. This will help you decide if you should work at a library!

Ask Questions!

Do you want to be a librarian? Ask your public librarian and school librarian what they like best about their jobs. Ask them what you should study in school. You will need a **graduate degree** to become a librarian.

GLOSSARY

borrow (BAR-oh) to take something that you plan to return later

clerks (KLURKS) library workers who do many tasks such as checking items in and out

director (duh-REK-tur) the head of an organization such as a library

graduate degree (GRAJ-oo-it dih-GREE) a title given by a college after a student finishes a specific set of classes; a degree earned after a bachelor's degree

librarians (lye-BRER-ee-uhnz) workers who have many jobs at the library such as helping people find books

library card (LYE-brer-ee KARD) a special card you can use to check out items from the library

research (REE-surch) careful study that is done to find information about something

scanner (SKAN-er) a tool that copies information into a computer

shelvers (SHELV-urz) workers who place books and other items on the library's shelves

sort (SORT) to separate or put things in a certain order

FIND OUT MORE

BOOKS

Garrett, Winston. *What Does a Library Media Specialist Do?* New York: PowerKids Press, 2015.

Murray, Julie. *Librarians*. Edina, MN: ABDO Kids, 2015.

WEB SITES

America's Story from America's Library
www.americaslibrary.gov/
Jump back in time with the Library of Congress to meet amazing Americans and discover the stories of America's past.

LibraryCareers—For Kids
http://librarycareers.drupalgardens.com/content/kids
Do you want to be a librarian? This Web Site will help you decide.

INDEX

ABOUT THE AUTHOR

Jennifer Colby is the author of many books for children. She always enjoyed going to the public library as a child. Now she is a librarian at a high school in Michigan. She enjoys taking her own children to the public library.